MomMom Cares

1st Edition

MomMom Cares

By Kira Turchin

Published by Kira Turchin
2883 Executive Park Drive
Suite 103
Weston, FL 33331

© 2015 Kira Turchin. All Rights Reserved.

MomMom Cares

ISBN-13: 978-0692376089
ISBN-10: 0692376089

No part of this book may be reproduced or utilized in any manner, form, or means, including print, digital, electronic, or mechanical means or methods, photocopying, recording, transcription, or stored or retrieved in and/or from any medium, without express written permission from the publishers.

Printed by CreateSpace
Designed by Jason Turchin

 Kira Turchin is a well-respected author, philanthropist, entrepreneur, biomedical engineer, wife, and most importantly, mommy. She is also the founder of the not-for-profit, Betty Cares, Inc., a charity benefitting parents of sick, injured and disabled children. More information can be found at www.BettyCares.org.

With a young child, Joshua, at home, and pregnant with her second child, Shaina, Kira experienced the untimely death of her mother, Betty. Betty was a heart-filled, joyous and supportive mother to Kira, mother-in-law to Jason, and a doting grandmother, or MomMom, to Kira's son. When Kira's son learned of MomMom's death, Kira turned to writing and art as a means of explaining their loss.

MomMom Cares delivers a positive message in the difficult times families may face when a loved one dies. "Whenever I see rainbows, I feel my mom's presence and feel as if she is watching over me," says Kira. "Whether it is rainbows, butterflies, lady bugs, or other positive signs, many people look to unexplained phenomena after losing a loved one, giving us a sense of comfort and reassurance, Since losing my mom, my family now always looks to rainbows to remind us that MomMom Betty Cares" adds Kira.

Dedication

This book is dedicated to my mom, Betty, known to my children as MomMom, and my wonderful husband, children and others caring for their loved ones. Together, may we continue to make a difference in the lives of caregivers.

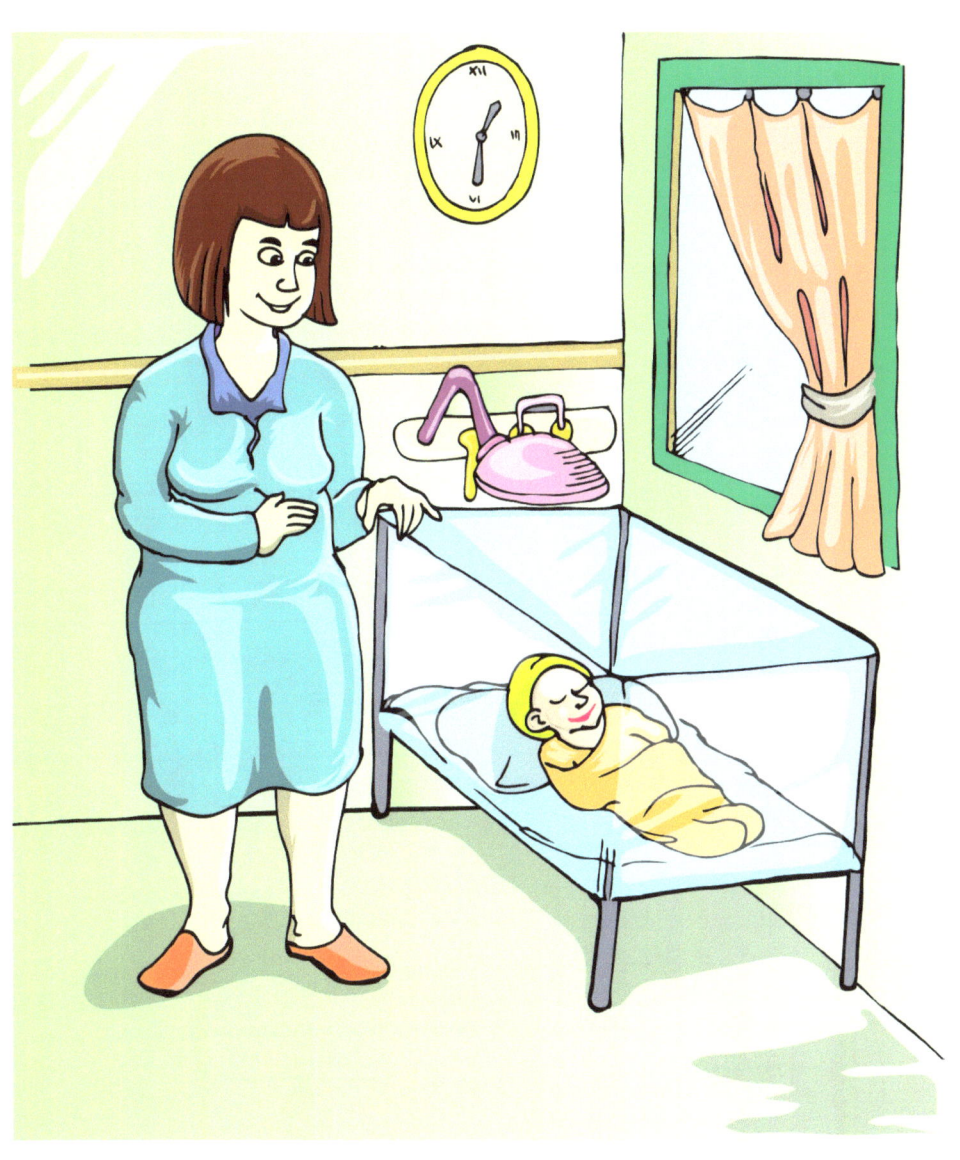

**When I was born,
I had a MomMom.**

I loved her very much.

My MomMom babysat all the time.

She got me to eat food when nobody else could.

She used to say, "Chew, Chew, Chew" and I would.

We laughed,

and we played.

We sang,

and we danced.

My MomMom cared about me.

My MomMom loved me.

My MomMom cared about my Mommy.

My MomMom loved her.

My MomMom cared about my Papa.

My MomMom loved him.

My MomMom cared about my Daddy.

My MomMom loved him too!

My MomMom loved animals.

She cared about them very much.

My MomMom loved music.

She used to sing a lot.

My MomMom loved rainbows.

She said they were special.

My MomMom is no longer with us.

I can no longer see MomMom.

I can no longer touch MomMom.

I can no longer hear MomMom's voice.

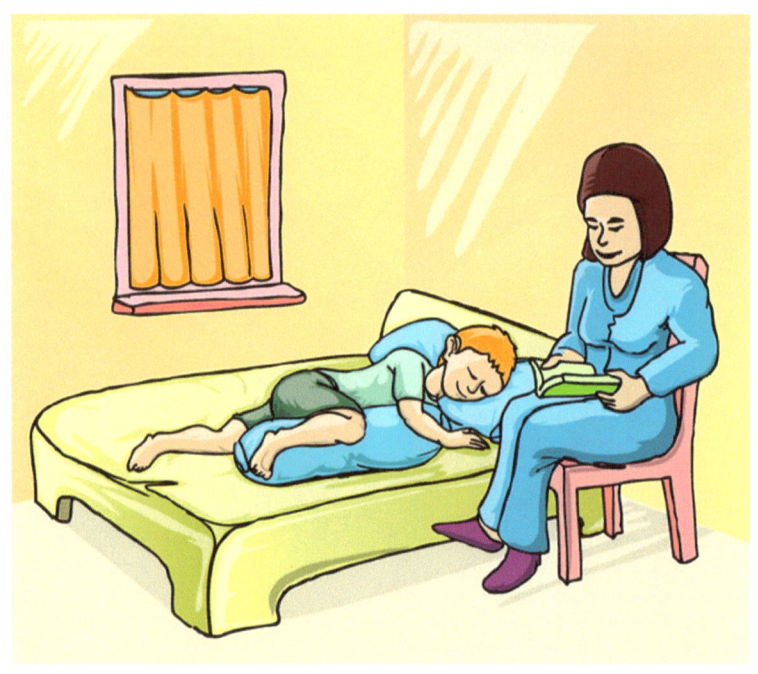

I can no longer feel MomMom's hugs and kisses.

But I know MomMom cares.

**MomMom lives in my heart.
She lives in my family's heart.**

She lives in the heart of everyone she cared about.

My Mommy told me that MomMom

would let us know that she is OK.

**Since she left us,
I see a lot of rainbows**

**when I think about
how much I miss her.**

So everytime I see a rainbow,

I know that MomMom cares.

www.ingramcontent.com/pod-product-compliance
Lightning Source LLC
Chambersburg PA
CBHW041745040426
42444CB00001B/37